A Cappella

An anthology of unaccompanied choral music
from seven centuries

Compiled and edited by

JOHN GARDNER and SIMON HARRIS

Music Department
OXFORD UNIVERSITY PRESS
Oxford and New York

Oxford University Press, Walton Street, Oxford OX2 6DP, England
Oxford University Press, 200 Madison Avenue, New York, NY 10016, USA

Oxford is a trade mark of Oxford University Press

The front cover design incorporates Adam Gumpelzhaimer's canon on the text 'Iubilate Deo'.
A transcription of the piece can be found on p. 51.

CONTENTS

PREFACE

It was as long ago as 1938 that I first had the idea of compiling an anthology of ensemble vocal music. I had been fired by the many collections issued by German publishers between the wars, which, if flawed by a chauvinism that caused *Now is the month of maying* to appear as *Nun strahlt der Mai den Herzen*, and Mozart's seductively amorous canon *V'amo di core teneramente* as the high-minded *Heilige Flamme, leucht uns empor*, were refreshingly free of the editorial clutter that was the norm in England at that time.

After the war, when I directed for many years a number of a cappella (that is, unaccompanied) amateur choirs—who, I insisted, should always sing songs in their original languages, however unwillingly—the need for a comprehensive, polyglot anthology became even more pressing: a volume which, instead of concentrating on, say, French chansons, Italian madrigals, or Tudor motets, would contain a representative collection of some of the best things we had sung, drawn from the music of more than one country, and covering many centuries of change and development.

There were several criteria to be observed in making my final choice for this anthology. There had to be pieces for a variety of ensembles, ranging from two to eight voices; a mixture of sacred and secular, of happy and sad pieces; and, above all, I had to have an intimate choirmaster's knowledge of each piece so that I could be sure that it would suit any group of singers prepared to enjoy reading through or rehearsing a wide range of musical styles. In order that it might be truly comprehensive, the collection would have to include some well-known 'standards' as well as lesser-known works. It would also have to contain examples of the many beautiful vocal canons written by great composers, for I had learnt early in my career as a choral singer and director that making polyphony out of a single line is the most flexible introduction that there is to a cappella music-making.

One absence from the anthology will be immediately apparent—the music of the twentieth century. There are many reasons for this: the first is that most of it is, at the time of writing, still in copyright; another, that the best examples tend to be very difficult to sing; yet another, that my own taste in this field is notoriously eccentric. It will also be seen that there is scanty representation of the music of the eighteenth century, a period which in its finest manifestations, such as the motets of Bach, ignored unaccompanied vocal polyphony in favour of mixed forces. I could, of course, have included an example of the English glee, but, except as a laborious means of raising a laugh, it is not a genre that I enjoy greatly.

As far as the production of this book is concerned, in general there has been a clear division of labour: I chose the contents and Simon Harris prepared the texts. There were two exceptions to this procedure. I had decided to include Josquin's eight-part motet *Tulerunt Dominum meum* without being aware first, that it also had been attributed to Nicholas Gombert; secondly, that it also existed as a setting of the text 'Lugebat David Absalon'; and thirdly, that it had a thematically linked sequel, *Porro rex operuit*. Likewise, I was unaware that Morley's two-part *Miraculous love's wounding* was a parody of Felice Anerio's four-part *Miracolo d'amore*. I agreed at once with Simon, who had given me this information, that the inclusion of the sequel to the Josquin/Gombert and the Anerio piece, both hitherto unknown to me, would greatly enhance the value of the collection.

All items appear with their original verbal texts. English translations have been added to no. 5, which might in music-hall parlance be described as a 'point number', and to no. 30, which might cause problems of diction for non-Scandinavian choirs. The musical texts appear without otiose editorial additions and suggestions; they are also presented in the composer's note values (with the exception of nos. 1 and 2 which might thereby prove troublesome) and at his own pitch. In this way an indication can be obtained of the kind of sonority originally envisaged, and choirs may be steered away from the now ubiquitous tendency to present all their music in SATB textures. On the other hand, by using the ranges placed at the beginning of each voice-part, it will nearly always be possible to find a key that is practicable for any group of voices that may propose to sing a particular work.

Though all the contents of this book can be sung a cappella, nos. 19, 20, and 21 have continuo lines, suggesting that they may have instrumental support of some kind. Though not indicated, this would certainly have also been the case in no. 22, and other works might well be performed with instruments, especially no. 17, which is delightfully apt for solo voice and four string-players. The possibilities of varied, mixed treatment are indeed endless, and the title of our anthology should not be taken to imply any dogmatic approach.

We should like to thank everyone who has helped us with the production of this anthology, but in particular: Professor Isabelle Cazeaux, Annamaria Garcia, Dr Edgar Hunt, Professor Brian Trowell, Nigel Wilson, and the Music Librarians of the Bristol Central Library, the Fitzwilliam Museum (Cambridge), and the Bayerische Staatsbibliothek, Munich.

JOHN GARDNER
December 1991

1. Sumer is icumen in
Perspice christicola

ANON.
(*c.*1280)

Sing cuc-cu nu,_____ Sing cuc-cu.

Sing cuc-cu. Sing cuc-cu nu,_____

Translation of the Latin instructions for performance: 'Four companions can sing this *rota*. It should not be sung by fewer than three or at least two, not counting those who sing the *pes*. It is sung in this way. While the others are silent one begins with those who sing the *pes*; when he gets to the first note after the cross the next begins; and so on. Each voice stops at the written pause marks—not elsewhere—and holds the last note for the duration of a [perfect] long [i.e. a dotted minim in transcription].
[For the *pes*, first part:] One person repeats this as many times as necessary, stopping at the end.
[For the *pes*, second part:] Another sings this, stopping [eventually] in the middle—not at the end. But [on getting to the end] going back straight away to the beginning.'
The pause marks mentioned in the instructions for the *rota* do not appear in the original, and have been supplied editorially.

2. Ave regina coelorum

GUILLAUME DUFAY
(*c.*1400–74)

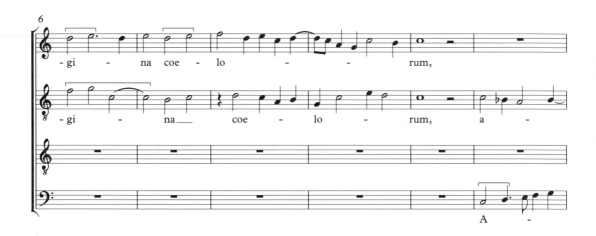

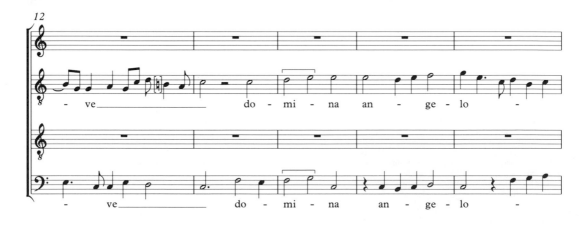

3. Ach herzigs Herz

HEINRICH FINCK
(1444/5–1527)

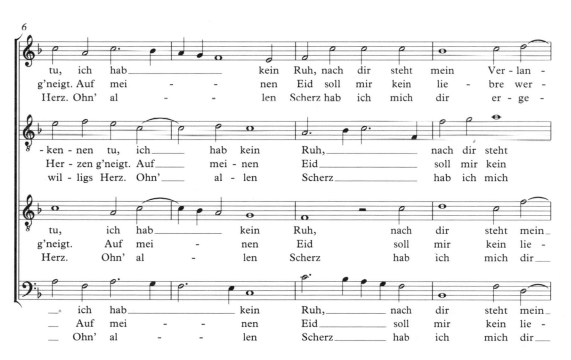

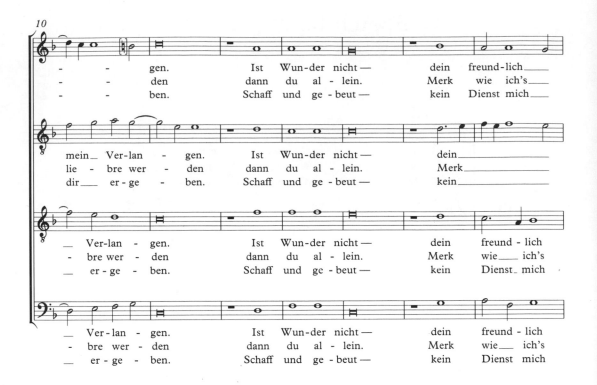

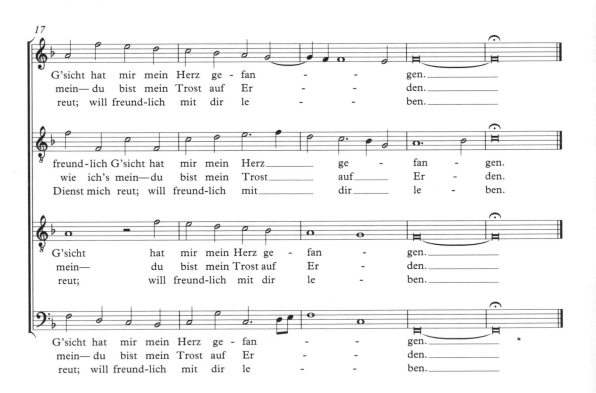

4. Puisqu'en amour a si grand passetemps

CLAUDIN DE SERMISY
(*c*.1490–1562)

5. Tri ciechi siamo

GIOVANNI DOMENICO DEL GIOVANE DA NOLA
(1510/20–1592)

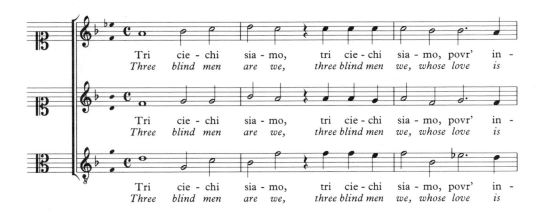

Tri cie-chi sia-mo, tri cie-chi sia-mo, povr' in-
Three blind men are we, three blind men we, whose love is

Tri cie-chi sia-mo, tri cie-chi sia-mo, povr' in-
Three blind men are we, three blind men we, whose love is

Tri cie-chi sia-mo, tri cie-chi sia-mo, povr' in-
Three blind men are we, three blind men we, whose love is

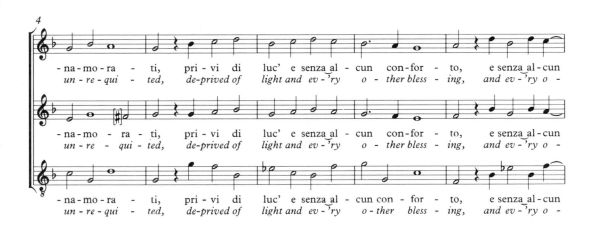

-na-mo-ra - ti, pri-vi di luc' e senza al-cun con-for - to, e senza al-cun
un-re-qui - ted, de-prived of light and ev-'ry o - ther bless - ing, and ev-'ry o-

-na-mo-ra - ti, pri-vi di luc' e senza al-cun con-for - to, e senza al-cun
un-re - qui - ted, de-prived of light and ev-'ry o - ther bless - ing, and ev-'ry o-

-na-mo-ra - ti, pri-vi di luc' e senza al-cun con - for - to, e senza al-cun
un-re-qui - ted, de-prived of light and ev-'ry o-ther bless - ing, and ev-'ry o-

__ con-for - to. Co - sì quel crud' A-mor___ sia fat - to tor - to, per
- ther bless - ing. O cru-el love our hearts___ you are op - press - ing by

con - for - to. Co - sì quel crud' A-mor___ sia fat - to tor - to, per
- ther bless-ing. O cru-el love our hearts___ you are op - press - ing by

__ con-for - to. Co - sì quel crud' A-mor___ sia fat - to tor - to, per
- ther bless - ing. O cru-el love our hearts___ you are op-press - ing by

6. Lugebat David Absalon

attributed to JOSQUIN DESPREZ
(*c*.1440–1521)
and to NICHOLAS GOMBERT
(*c*.1495–*c*.1560)

Prima Pars

Secunda Pars: Porro rex operuit

7. Los braços traygo cansados

JUAN VASQUEZ
(*c*.1510–*c*.1560)

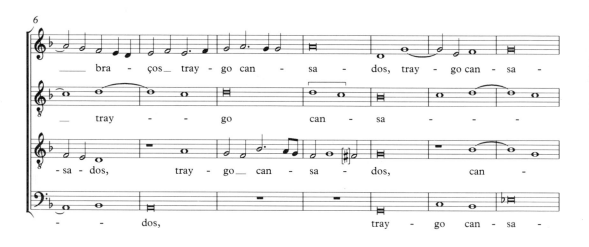

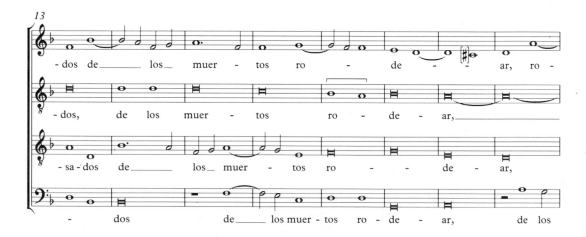

8. La nuit froide et sombre

ORLANDE DE LASSUS
(1532–1594)

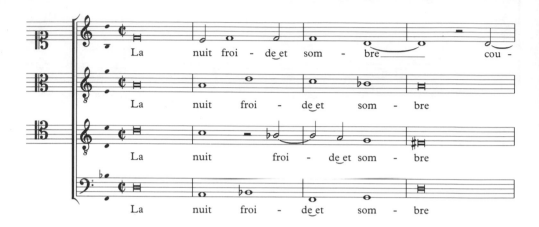

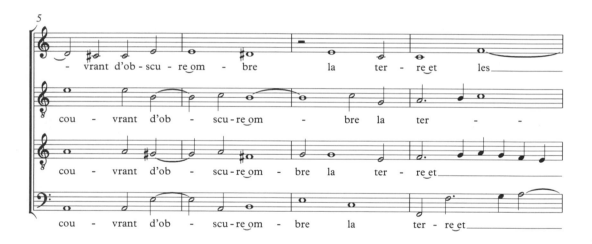

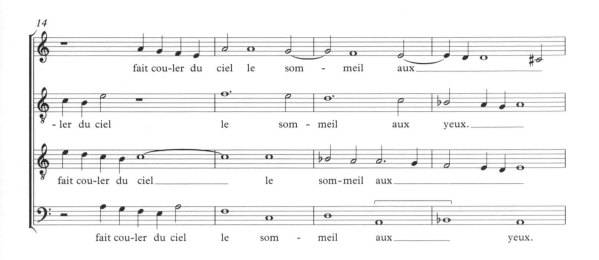

9. Laetentur coeli

WILLIAM BYRD
(1543–1623)

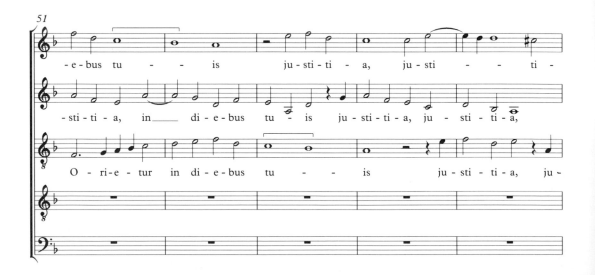

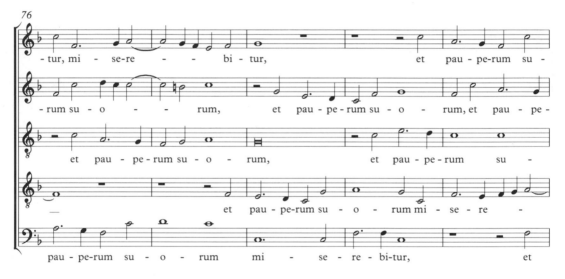

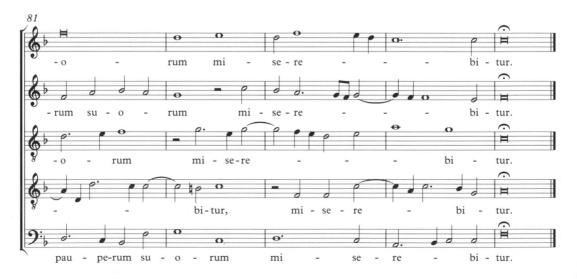

10. Miracolo d'amore

FELICE ANERIO
(c.1560–1614)

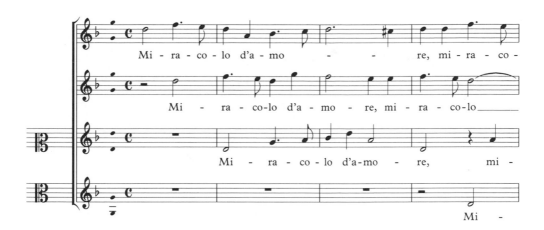

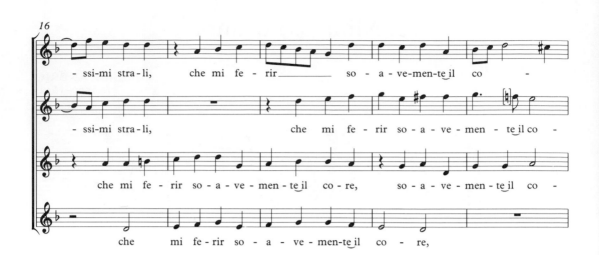

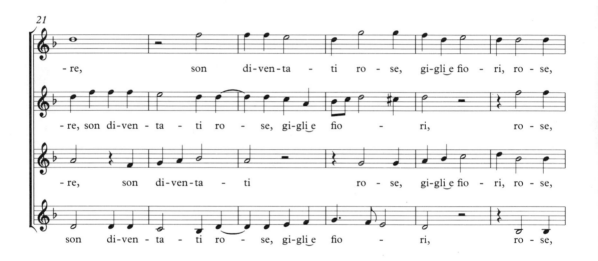

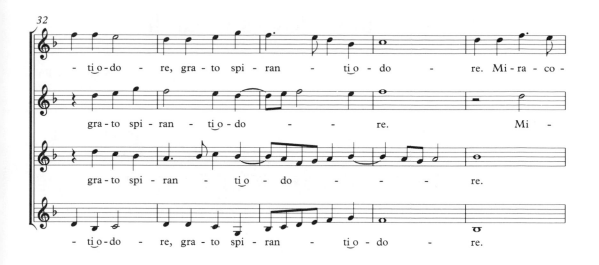

11. Miraculous love's wounding

THOMAS MORLEY
(1557/8–1602)

12. Benedictus qui venit

(from *Missa Ad Fugam*)

GIOVANNI PIERLUIGI DA PALESTRINA
(1525/6–94)

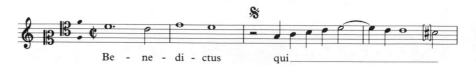

Be – ne – di – ctus qui_____

ve – – – nit_____ in no – mi – ne__

__ Do – mi – ni,_____ Do – mi – ni, in

no – mi – ne Do – mi – ni,_____ Do – mi – ni.

This is a three-part canon in which each voice enters a perfect fifth below the previous one. We give the three original clefs which indicate this. Each part should be read in the treble clef once the correct starting pitch has been found, though the following two minor adjustments have to be made: the two editorial B♭s in bar 6 should only be sung by the top part, and the semibreve F in bar 13 should be sung as an F♯ by the lowest part. We have included signs indicating the points of entry (𝄋) and conclusion (⌢) of the two lower parts, as in the original.

13. Iubilate Deo

ADAM GUMPELZHAIMER
(1559–1625)

Iu - bi - la - te De - o om - nis ter - - ra: ser - vi - te

Do - mi - no,   ser - vi - te Do - mi - no in lae - ti - ti - a.

This is an infinite five-part canon at the unison, each voice entering after a space of three semibreves as shown by the original entry signs.

14. She weepeth sore

WILLIAM LAWES
(1602–1645)

She   wee - peth sore   in the   night,   and her   tears___

___ are on   her cheek.___ Her priests sigh and her vir - gins are af -

- flic-ted,   and a - mong___ all her   lo - vers she_____ hath__ none to com - fort her.

This is an infinite four-part canon at the unison, each voice entering at two-bar intervals as shown by the original sign for the second entry.

15. Draw on, sweet night

JOHN WILBYE
(1574–1638)

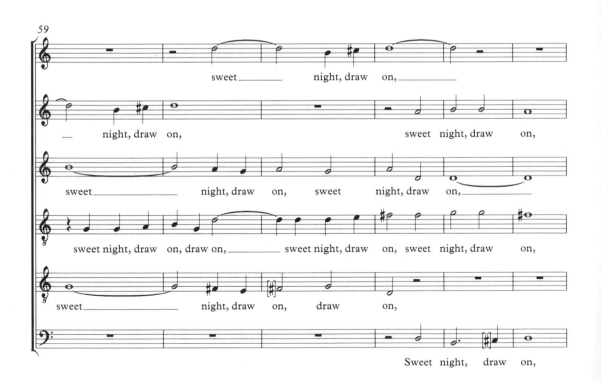

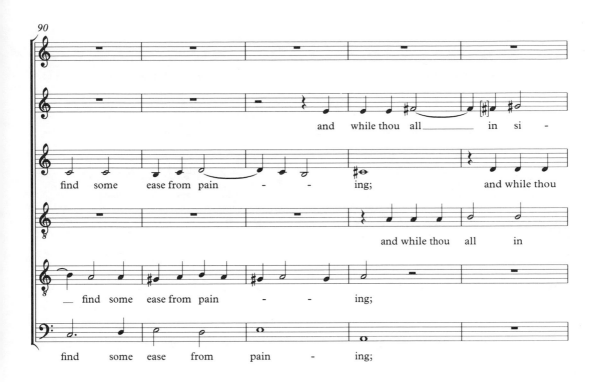

16. Dolcissima mia vita

CARLO GESUALDO
(*c.*1561–1613)

17. The Silver Swan

ORLANDO GIBBONS
(1583–1625)

11

shore,   thus sung her first   and   last, and sung   no more:

sung her first   and last, and sung   no more, no_____   more: 'Fare - well all

thus sung her   first____ and_ last,   and   sung   no   more: 'Fare -

first and last, and   sung no   more, and sung____   no____   more: 'Fare -

thus sung   her   first and   last,   and   sung   no   more: 'Fare - well all

15

'Fare - well all   joys,   O   death come close   mine

joys,   O_____ death   come close   mine   eyes.   More

- well all   joys,   O   death   come_____ close mine eyes.

- well   all   joys,_ O   death   come close   mine

joys,   O   death come close   mine   eyes.

18

eyes.   More   geese than   swans   now   live,   more fools   than wise.'

geese than swans   now   live,   more   fools   than wise,   than_____   wise.'

More geese than   swans____   now_ live,   more   fools   than   wise.'

eyes. More geese than   swans now   live, more fools____   than____   wise.'

More geese   than   swans now   live,   more   fools   than   wise.'

18. Der Kuckuck

JOHANN STEFFENS
(*c*.1560–1616)

19. Jesu, dulcis memoria

RICHARD DERING
(*c.*1580–1630)

20. Gaudete omnes

JAN PIETERSZOON SWEELINCK
(1562–1621)

112

119

21. Ich bin eine rufende Stimme

HEINRICH SCHÜTZ
(1585–1672)

22. Hear my prayer, O Lord

HENRY PURCELL
(1659–1695)

23. Wo der perlender Wein

WOLFGANG AMADEUS MOZART
(1756–91)

Wo der per-len-der Wein im Gla-se blinkt, da

lasst uns wei - - - len.

This is a six-part infinite canon, Mozart's score (lacking both clefs and key-signatures) indicating the first two voices to enter as sopranos, the remaining four as tenors singing an octave lower. This gives a bare unresolved perfect fourth at the second entry, which may be avoided if the first entry lies an octave below the second; thereafter it seems to us to make little difference whether subsequent entries are for sopranos or tenors. For a full choir we suggest transposing the canon down a major third into B flat, and adopting the following order of voices: B2 A S1 T S2 B1.

24. Tod und Schlaf

FRANZ JOSEPH HAYDN
(1732–1809)

Tod ist ein lan - ger Schlaf. Schlaf ist ein kur-zer, kur-zer

Tod, der lin-dert dir, und je-ner tilgt des Le-bens Not! Tod ist ein lan - ger Schlaf.

25. Lacrimoso son io

FRANZ SCHUBERT
(1797–1825)

a) *First Version*

La - cri - mo - so, la - cri - mo - so son i - o,— son—
i - o, la - cri - mo - so, la - cri - mo - so son i - o,— son i -
- o, la - cri - mo - so, la - cri - mo - so son— i - o,— son i - o, i - o.

b) *Second Version*

La - cri - mo - sa, la - cri - mo - sa son i - o,— son i -
- o, la - cri - mo - sa, la - cri - mo - sa son i - o,— son— i - o, la - cri -
- mo - sa,— la - cri - mo - sa son— i - o, son i - o, i - o.

26. Wenn Kummer hätte zu töten Macht

JOHANNES BRAHMS
(1833–97)

Andante espressivo

Wenn Kum - mer hät - te— zu tö - ten, zu tö - ten Macht,—
— er müss - te töt - lich dies Herz durch boh - ren; und liess— ein Gluck sich zu -
- rück - beschwö - ren, mein Seuf - zen hätt' es zu - rück - be - schwö - ren.

27. An den Sturmwind

Rasch und kräftig
Allegro energico

PETER CORNELIUS
(1824–74)

28. Christus factus est

ANTON BRUCKNER
(1824–96)

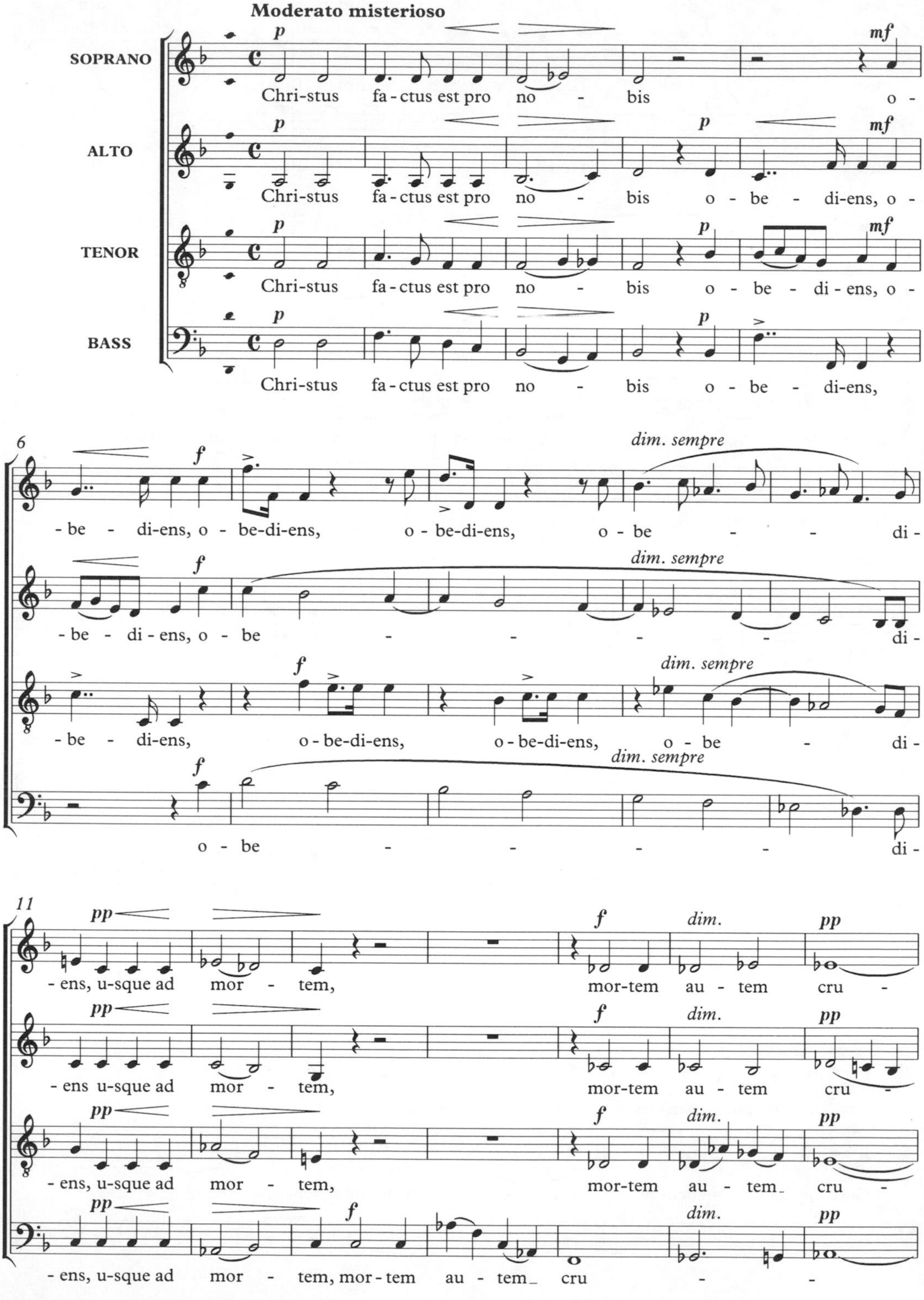

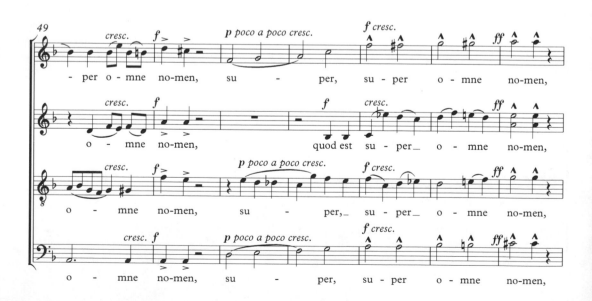

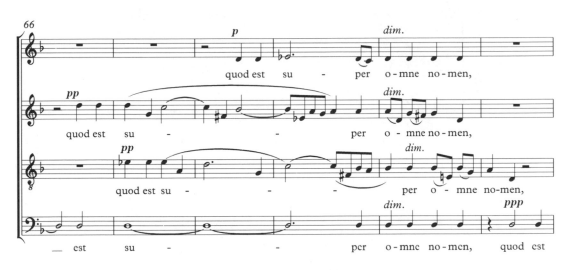

29. Beati quorum via

CHARLES VILLIERS STANFORD
(1852–1924)

30. Guds Sön har gjort mig fri

EDWARD GRIEG
(1843–1907)

Tempo I, animato

EDITORIAL NOTES

Pitch. All pieces are shown at the pitch at which they appear in the primary source consulted. We suggest that choirs should transpose pieces to pitches suited to their voices whenever necessary.

Clefs, voice ranges, and voice names. Treble, octave treble, and bass clefs only are used in our transcriptions. Original clefs (where they differ from ours) are shown at the beginning of each piece, as is the original range of each voice. But because the meanings of voice names have changed over the centuries, original voice names are not generally given.

Note values. In all pieces except nos. 1 and 2 our transcriptions preserve the original note values. In the first two pieces the opening notes of the primary source consulted are shown in our transcription immediately after the original clefs.

Triple proportion and ligatures. In transcribing triple proportion we have used triplets rather than changes of time, since they seem to us less ambiguous. Ligatures are shown by square brackets above the stave, in the normal manner.

Tempo, style, and expression. Editorial indications for the tempo and style of a piece seem to be commonplace in modern publications of choral music. We feel that they are as unnecessary here as they would be in instrumental music, and so we have added as little as possible to whatever instructions appear in primary sources about how a piece is to be performed. All slurs, dynamics, and expression marks are original, and what little else we have added appears in square brackets.

Accidentals. Accidentals that appear in the primary source are printed at the normal size in front of the note. Many original accidentals turn out to be unnecessary when a piece is barred in modern notation; most of these have been omitted without comment, but we have retained what seem to us to be useful clarifications or reminders, and added a few of our own in square brackets where we think there can be no doubt about the sense of the original. Square brackets are also used for the application of *musica ficta*.

Verbal texts and translations. In all but two of the pieces in this collection (nos. 5 and 30) the only words given with the music are those of the primary source. Where they are not English, a prose translation is given below in the notes on the piece. Except in the case of the medieval English text of no. 1, spelling has been modernized where possible. All references to the Bible are to the Authorized Version of the English Bible. As far as possible, word underlay follows that of the original, but where the latter is unclear or obviously wrong, editorial changes have been made without comment.

We have decided that the language of the words of

no. 30 is sufficiently unfamiliar to English-speaking choirs for us to supply an English singing translation. We have also provided one for no. 5, because of the theatrical character of the text.

Basso Continuo. Beyond correcting what seemed to us absolutely necessary, we have left the original continuo parts in nos. 19, 20, and 21 as they stand. These pieces may be, and frequently are, performed successfully without continuo, but if the continuo is used it may leave many uncertainties which performers must resolve (like, for example, the opening chord of no. 19).

Notes on individual pieces

The notes that follow on each piece show show: (*i*) the primary source consulted; (*ii*) any facsimiles of this or other primary sources published in a modern edition known to us; (*iii*) modern editions of the piece that list the primary sources for it and/or give a critical commentary for it; (*iv*) the source of the words for the piece (if it can be identified); (*v*) an English prose translation of its text if necessary; and (*vi*) any further information about the piece that seems to us of interest.

The term 'original' used above refers to the primary source consulted. In some cases there are several primary sources from which to choose, in others the only known primary source has itself disappeared and we are dependent on a modern edition. In most cases it cannot be assumed that the primary source consulted was produced under the composer's supervision or reflects his final intentions.

A few brief critical commentaries are provided for those pieces for which the musical text of the primary source consulted needs amendment, and for which we give no reference to a critical commentary in a modern edition. The reference system used here is as follows: bar number, voice number (counting down from top line); note number (counting tied notes separately); reading of primary source.

1. Sumer is icumen in / *Perspice christicola* (Anon., c.1280)

Primary source: British Library (London, Brit. Mus.) MS Harley 978 (RISM no. LoHa), fo. 11ᵛ. Facsimile: *Grove's Dictionary of Music*, 5th ed. (1954), Vol. VII, frontispiece (in colour).

This four-part infinite canon at the unison (*rota*) accompanied by a two-part rondellus (*pes*) has been printed in countless modern editions. Its date of origin seems no longer to be a matter of dispute. Controversy nowadays focuses on whether the English or the Latin text is the original, and whether or not the apparent erasures in the MS are evidence that the piece was originally in binary metre.

The singing instructions in the MS are as follows.

For the *rota*: 'Hanc rotam cantare possunt quatuor socii. a paucioribus autem quam a tribus vel saltem duobus non debet dici, preter eos qui dicunt pedem. canitur autem sic. tacentibus ceteris unus inchoat cum hiis qui tenent pedem. et cum venerit ad primam notam post crucem, inchoat alius. et sic de ceteris. singuli vero repausent ad pausaciones scriptas et non alibi, spacio unius longe note.'

For the *pes* (1st part): 'Hoc repetit unus quociens opus est, faciens pausacionem in fine.' (2nd part): 'Hoc dicit alius, pausans in medio et non in fine. sed immediate repetens principium.'

We have supplied editorially the pause marks mentioned in the instructions for the *rota*, since they do not appear in the MS. The source of neither text is known.

Translations. (*i*) Medieval English: Summer has come, loudly sing cuckoo. The seed grows, the meadow blooms and the wood comes to life. Sing cuckoo. The ewe bleats for the lamb, the cow lows for the calf, the bullock starts, the buck farts. Merrily sing cuckoo. Cuckoo, cuckoo, much do you sing cuckoo—don't stop now. (*ii*) Latin: See, Christian, what an honour this is. The heavenly farmer has not spared his son, but has exposed him to destruction for the sake of the blemish on the vine. And he restores to life the half-living prisoners from their punishment, and crowns them with him on the throne of heaven.

2. Ave regina coelorum (Dufay)

Primary source: Biblioteca Vaticana (Rome) MS S. Pietro B.80, fos. 25ᵛ–27ʳ. Facsimile (partial): *Corpus Mensurabilis Musicae*, Series 1, Vol. 5 after p. xlv. Transcribed in *Guillaume Dufay: Opera Omnia* (*Corpus Mensurabilis Musicae*, Series 1) Vol. 5 (*Minor Liturgical Compositions*), ed. Heinrich Besseler (1966) pp. 124–30. With critical commentary, p. xlii.

S. Pietro B.80, the only source for this piece, was copied for Cambrai Cathedral, and has been confidently dated 1464. So although the text suggests that Dufay composed this work on his deathbed, he must have written it at least ten years before he died. But on stylistic grounds it is thought to be one of the latest surviving works by him.

The words are those of the Marian Antiphon 'Ave regina coelorum', of which the plainsong also appears, somewhat changed, in the Tenor part, to be sung at Compline between the Feast of the Purification and Maundy Thursday. Into this text is woven that of a specially composed trope (which the Tenor voice does not sing), praying for Dufay's soul.

Translation: (Antiphon) Hail, Queen of Heaven, hail, Mistress of the Angels,/(Trope) Have mercy upon thy failing Dufay, lest he perish in the hot fire of his sins./(A.) Hail, holy root, from which light has arisen upon the world./(T.) Have mercy upon us, Mother of God, so that the gate of heaven will be open to the sick man./(A.) Rejoice, O glorious one, above all mankind fair./(T.) Have mercy upon the supplicant Dufay, that his death may be agreeable in your sight./(A.) Farewell, O truly beautiful one, and pray always to

Christ on our behalf./(T.) Have mercy upon us, that we be not condemned on high, and help us, that in the hour of death our hearts may be acceptable.

3. Ach herzigs Herz (Finck)

Primary source: *Schöne auszerlesene Lieder des hoch berümpten Heinrici Finckens . . .* , Formschneider, Nürnberg 1536 (RISM no. 1536⁹). Transcribed in *Heinrich Finck: Ausgewählte Werke*, Vol. 2 (*Das Erbe Deutscher Musik*, Vol. 70), ed. Lothar Hoffmann–Erbrecht and Helmut Lomnitzer (1981), pp. 146–7. With critical commentary pp. 201–2.

The composer of this lied was one of the best known contemporaries of Josquin, but its words are anonymous.

Translation: 1. Ah, dearest heart, you know my pain. I have no rest, for all my desire is for you; and no wonder—your sweet face has captured my heart. 2. Now that I regard you with such heartfelt longing, upon my oath I could not love anyone but you. Take note of how I feel—you are my earthly solace. 3. Accept the gift of my willing heart, for—and I do not jest—I have surrendered myself to you. Act and command; no service shall I repent, but will live with you in devotion.

4. Puisqu'en amour (Sermisy)

Primary source: *Trente-et-une chansons musicales a quatre parties . . .* , Attaingnant, Paris 1529 (RISM no. 1529²). Transcribed in *Sermisy: Opera Omnia* (*Corpus Mensurabilis Musicae*, Series 52), Vol. 4 (*Chansons*), ed. Isabelle Cazeaux (1974), pp. 64–6, with a note on the sources, p. xii.

Another secular song by a well-known composer, with anonymous words. The second verse does not appear in Attaingnant's print, but is to be found in *Sensuyvent plusieurs belles chansons* (Anon.), 1537, fo. 18.

Translation: 1. Because love is so fine a pastime, I feel like loving, singing, dancing, and laughing in order to lighten my heart, which sorrow now torments. That is the aim I have, the end I seek. 2. If I have the love of her whom I claim, believe me, boredom and care (which is worse) will not be able to worry me, because I shall be one of those who are happy.

8.4.2: ♩B

5. Tri ciechi siamo (Nola)

Primary source: *Canzone vilanesche . . . a tre voci*, Libro I° (Libro 2°) Gardano, Venice 1545 (RISM no. N774). Transcribed in *Giovanni Domenico del Giovane da Nola: Madrigali e Canzoni Villanesche* Vol. 1, ed. Lionello Cammarota (1973), pp. 124–5, with footnotes.

For the kinds of occasion on which this *mascherata* may have been performed, see Alfred Einstein; *The Italian Madrigal* (1947), vol. 1, p. 366.

6. Lugebat David Absalon (attrib. Josquin/Gombert)

Primary source: *Thesaurus Musicus continens selectissimas 8, 7, 6, 5 et 4 vocum Harmonias, tam a veteris quam recentioribus symphonistis compositus...*, Montanus and Neuber, Nürnberg 1564 (RISM no. 1564[1]).

As far as we know, the *Thesaurus Musicus* is the only place where the two parts of this motet appear together as part of the same piece, where they are attributed to Josquin. Both parts appear elsewhere. The first was published with the text 'Tulerunt Dominum mcum' by Montanus and Neuber in 1554, where it is also attributed to Josquin, and it was from this publication that Blume prepared his edition of the first part for *Das Chorwerk*, Vol. 23 (1950; pp. 22–8 with critical notes on p. 3). The first part also appears in two MS sources with the texts 'Je prens congie' and 'Sustinuimus pacem', being attributed on both occasions to Gombert. The second part appears anonymously as an independent piece in the same MS as *Sustinuimus pacem* (Verona, Accademia Filarmonica no. 218) with the text 'Tu sola es virgo' (see *The New Grove Dictionary of Music and Musicians*, 1980, Vol. 9, p. 735). Neither part appears in the publication of the collected works of either composer, and as far as we know the second part is here published in a modern edition for the first time.

More important, perhaps, than the issue of authorship, is whether the two parts really belong together. In three of the voices there are significant differences in range between the two parts, the first part is distinctly more imitative than the second, and only one source out of four shows them as two parts of the same work. Against this, the second part does not appear at all in two of the other three sources, both parts are in the same mode and they sound similar because they contain closely similar passages of music.

Translation: (1st part) David mourned for Absalom as a loving father for his son, as an old man for a youth. 'Alas, my son Absalom, would that I could die for you!' King David wept for his son with covered head. (2nd part) Later the king covered his head and cried in a loud voice: 'O my son Absalom!'

(1st part) 39.3: o E, ♩♩♩♩ A B C D / 40.3: o o C D; (2nd part) 4.4.2, 3: ♩♩ E D / 5.4.1: o C / 20.5.1 : ♩ D / 28.7.2: ♩♩ D C / 30–2.1: one bar's rest missing / 40.3.1, 2: ♮ C / 44.3.1, 2: ♮ C / 45.6.1 : ♩ E / 60.6.1: ♩ G omitted / 60.6.6: ♮ D / 61–2.1 : tie omitted / 66.3.1, 2: o B flat / 67–70.6 : 2 bars' rest omitted.

7. Los braços traygo cansados (Vasquez)

Primary source: *Recopilación de sonetos y villancicos a 4 y a 5*, Seville 1560 (Madrid: Biblioteca de la Casa Ducal de Medinaceli nos. 13133–7). Transcribed in *Juan Vasquez: Recopilación de sonetos y villancicos a 4 y a 5*, 1560 (*Monumentos de la Musica Española*, Vol. 4), ed. H. Anglés (1946), pp. 193–4, with footnotes.

In Valderrábano's arrangement for voice and vihuela of this piece (*Silva de Sirenas*, 1547, *Monumentos de la Musica Española*, Vol. 22, pp. 36–7) the cantus-firmus-like Altus part appears as the voice part.

The text is lines 17–20 (apparently slightly altered) of the anonymous *Romance de la muerte de Don Beltrán*, published in R. Menendez Pidal, *Flor Nueva de Romances Viejos que recogió de la tradición antigua y moderna*, Madrid 1928, pp. 106–9. The same text appears in a three-part setting as no. 446 of the *Cancionero de Palacio*.

Translation: I raise my weary arms from going round the dead, I see all the French, but I don't see Don Beltrán.

8. La Nuit Froide et Sombre (Lassus)

Primary source: *Les Meslanges d'Orlande de Lassus contenantz plusieurs chansons à 4, 5, 6, 8 et 10 parties*, Le Roy et Ballard, Paris 1576 (RISM no. L891). Transcribed in *Orlando di Lasso: Sämtliche Werke*, 1st Series, vol. 12, ed. F. X. Haberl and A. Sandberger (1894–1953), pp. 34–5, with critical commentary p. xlix.

The words are from a poem by Joachim du Bellay (1522–60).

Translation: The cold and sombre night, covering earth and sky with its dark shadow, makes honey-sweet sleep fall from heaven on to our eyes. Then dawning day, leading us to work, shows its light, and in diverse colours adorns and shapes the great universe.

9. Laetentur coeli (Byrd)

Primary Source: *Liber Primus Sacrarum Cantionum*, Thomas Este, London 1589 (RISM no. B 5211).

The words of this motet are taken from a Responsory for Matins for the first Monday in Advent (in the Catholic rite). The music takes its form from that of the Responsory; it is in two parts, the second part (beginning with the words 'Orietur in diebus tuis') corresponding to the verse of the Responsory. The same 17 bars of music conclude both parts because they set the end of the respond ('et pauperum suorum miserebitur') which is repeated at the end of the verse.

Translation: Let the heavens rejoice and the earth be merry. Be joyful, O mountains, give praise; for our Lord will come and take pity upon his poor people. Justice will arise in thy days, and there will be an abundance of peace. And he will take pity upon his poor people.

10. Miracolo d'amore (Anerio)

Primary source: *Canzonette a Quattro Voci*, Lib. I° 5th ed., Vincenzi and Amadino, Venice 1607 (RISM no. A1089).

We have included this piece mainly because comparison with the next will show the extent to which Morley's two-part canzonets depend upon Anerio's four-part canzonets (1st ed. 1586), not only for their texts but also for their musical ideas (see particularly Joseph Kerman, *The Elizabethan Madrigal: a comparative study*, New York 1962, pp. 159–63). The text is anonymous.

Translation: Miracle of love, your sharpest darts,

which pierce my heart so gently, are become sweet-scented roses, lilies, flowers. Miracle of love.

30.1.1: ♩ D; preceding rest omitted.

11. Miraculous love's wounding (Morley)

Primary source: *The First Book of Canzonets to Two Voyces,* Thomas Este, London 1595 (RISM no. M3701). Facsimile: *Morley's Canzonets for Two Voices,* ed. John E. Uhler, Baton Rouge, 1954.
The anonymous text of this canzonet appears in *English Madrigal Verse,* ed. E. H. Fellowes, 3rd ed., Oxford 1967, p. 145.

12. Benedictus qui venit (Palestrina)

Primary Source: *Liber Secundus Missarum,* V. and A. Dorico, Rome 1567 (RISM no. P660).
This Benedictus comes from the Sanctus of Palestrina's *Missa Ad Fugam.*
Translation: Blessed be he that cometh in the name of the Lord. (Psalm 118: 26a)
1.1: time signature ¢

13. Iubilate Deo (Gumpelzhaimer)

Primary source: *Compendium Musicae,* 6th ed., J. U. Schönig, Augsburg 1616, fo. 31ᵛ (RISM no. 1616²³).
Translation: O be joyful in God all ye lands: serve the Lord with gladness. (Psalm 100:1)

14. She weepeth sore (W. Lawes)

Primary source: *Catch that catch can,* John Hilton, London 1652, p. 107 (RISM no. 1652¹⁰).
Lefkowitz observes (Murray Lefkowitz, *William Lawes,* London 1960, p. 247) that this is a religious canon, with a text from Lamentations I: 2a, 4b, 2b.

15. Draw on, sweet night (Wilbye)

Primary source: *The Second Set of Madrigals to 3, 4, 5 and 6 parts . . .,* Thomas Este, London 1609 (RISM no. W1066). Facsimile: *English Madrigals 1588–1630* ed. F. W. Sternfeld and David Greer, no. 46: *John Wilbye: The Second Set of Madrigals,* The Scolar Press, Menston 1972.
The anonymous text of this madrigal appears in *English Madrigal Verse,* ed. E. H. Fellowes, 3rd ed., Oxford 1967, pp. 317–8.

16. Dolcissima mia vita (Gesualdo)

Primary source: *Partitura delli Sei Libri de' Madrigali a Cinque Voci . . . ,* Simone Molinaro, Genoa 1613 (RISM no. G1743). This madrigal, No. 4 of Book 5, sets an anonymous text.
Translation: My sweetest life, why do you delay the help I long for? Do you perhaps believe that the sweet fire that consumes me will be extinguished just because you avert your gaze? Alas! May it never be that my desire inspires the wish either to love you or to die!

17. The Silver Swan (Gibbons)

Primary source: *The First Set of Madrigals and Mottets of Five Parts,* Thomas Snodham, London 1612

(RISM no. G1994). The anonymous words of this madrigal appear in *English Madrigal Verse,* ed. E. H. Fellowes, 3rd ed., Oxford 1967, p. 110. We have amended the celebrated augmented triad at the beginning of bars 10 and 17, which we think is probably wrong, by altering the first E flat in the third part to D in each case.

10.3.1: ♩ E flat / 17.3.1: ♩ E flat

18. Der Kuckuck (Steffens)

Primary source: *Neue Teutsche Weltliche Madrigalia und Balletten . . . von Johann Stephan,* Heinrich Cartens, Hamburg 1618/9 (RISM no. S5751). Transcribed in *Johann Steffens: Neue Teutsche Weltliche Madrigalia und Balletten* (*Das Erbe Deutscher Musik,* Vol. 29, part 2), ed. Gustav Fock, Wolfenbüttel 1958, pp. 99–101, with critical commentary p. 110.
The above publication of Steffens' Ballets was prepared from Gustav Fock's transcription, made in 1935 from a primary source now partly lost. The text is anonymous.
Translation: The cuckoo has fallen to his death from a high willow tree. Fa la la . . . Who will now beguile us through the long year? My darling has sent me a letter in which it is written that she has taken another lover and has abandoned me. That she left me does not trouble me much, for no one should stay who wishes to go. I have a mind that pays little regard to such things.

19. Jesu, dulcis memoria (Dering)

Primary source: *Cantiones Sacrae Quinque Vocum cum Basso Continuo ad Organum,* Phalèse, Antwerp 1617. 2nd ed., ibid. 1634 (RISM nos. D1317, D1318).
This is a setting of a text by St Bernard of Clairvaux (1091–1153). For the purposes of the critical notes below, the two editions are identical.
Translation: Jesus, of sweet memory, gives true joy to the heart. Even above honey and all things is his presence sweet. Nothing more agreeable is sung, nothing happier is heard, nothing sweeter is thought than Jesus, son of God.
9–10.2: tie omitted / b.c. 48: ○ E sharp / 49.5.2: ♩ C / 65.2: whole bar omitted

20. Gaudete omnes (Sweelinck)

Primary source: *Cantiones Sacrae Quinque Vocum cum Basso Continuo ad Organum,* Phalèse, Antwerp 1619 (RISM no. S7252).
Although this piece appears in the Sweelinck *Opera Omnia* (Vol. 6, Amsterdam 1957), we have supplied a slightly different text here (see critical notes below). The anonymous text of this motet indicates that it was destined for Advent or Christmas.
Translation: Rejoice, everyone, and be merry; for lo, the wished for one is come. Enter into his sight with joy. Know that he himself is the one we await. Alleluia.
11.5 & b.c. 2: ♩ A / 49.b.c.3: ♩ B/97.3.4,5: ♫ FE

21. Ich bin eine rufende Stimme (Schütz)

Primary source: *Musicalia ad Chorum Sacrum, id est*

Geistliche Chormusik mit 5, 6 und 7 Stimmen . . . Op. 11, Johann Klemm, Dresden 1648 (RISM no. S2294).

Translation: I am a voice crying in the wilderness: Make straight the way of the Lord. I baptize with water, but there walks one among you whom you know not. He it is who will come after me, yet was before me, whose shoe-laces I am not worthy to unloose. (John I : 23–7)

11.b.c.1,2: figuring 6 7 over note 1, 7 6 over note 2/

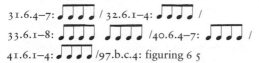

41.6.1–4: ♩♩♩ /97.b.c.4: figuring 6 5

22. Hear my prayer, O Lord (Purcell)

Primary source: Fitzwilliam Museum (Cambridge), MS 88 fo. 83$^{r–v}$. Transcribed in *Purcell Society Edition*, Vol. 28 (*Sacred Music*, Part 4) ed. Anthony Lewis and Nigel Fortune (1959, rev. 1967), pp. 135–8, with critical commentary p. 194.

This short piece is almost certainly no more than the opening of what was intended to be a substantial motet (see Franklin B. Zimmerman, *Henry Purcell (1659–95): an Analytical Catalogue of his Music*, London 1963, p. 14). The text is Psalm 102: 1.

23. Wo der perlender Wein (Mozart)

Primary Source: Mozarteum (Salzburg), MS 27. Transcribed in *W. A. Mozart: Neue Ausgabe Sämtlicher Werke*, Series III, Vol. 10, ed. Albert Dunning, Kassel 1974, pp. 84–5.

The critical commentary for the music in this volume is still to be issued by the publisher. The piece is thought to date from 1782, shortly after Mozart's arrival in Vienna (See H. Abert, *W. A. Mozart*, 7th ed., Leipzig 1956, Vol. 2, p. 53). The text we give appears for the first time in *W. A. Mozarts Werke*, Leipzig 1877–1905, Series 7, no. 48, Vol. 2, p. 15. Köchel supplies another similarly convivial one (*Chronologisch-thematisches Verzeichnis sämtlicher Tonwerke W. A. Mozarts*, 7th ed., Wiesbaden 1965, pp. 399–400). The original MS is textless.

Translation: Where the sparkling wine twinkles in the glass, there let us linger.

24. Tod und Schlaf (Haydn)

Primary source: Österreichische Nationalbibliothek (Vienna), MS 15966. Transcribed in *Joseph Haydn: Werke*, Series XXXI, ed. O. E. Deutsch, Munich 1959, p. 42 (with critical commentary in separate booklet, pp. 16–20, 28).

This is a four-part infinite canon at the unison, probably written sometime in the 1790s. We give it at the pitch of the source above, which is not that of the Collected Edition. The text is an epigram by Friedrich von Logau (1604–55).

Translation: Death is a long sleep; sleep a short death, which soothes you and blots out life's trouble.

25. Lacrimoso son io (Schubert)

Primary sources: Two MSS, one dated August 1815;

both now lost. First published in *Franz Schuberts Werke*, Leipzig 1884–97, Series 19, no. 28. Transcribed in *Franz Schubert, Neue Gesamtausgabe*, Series III, Vol. 4, ed. Dietrich Berke, Kassel 1974, pp. 40–1, with critical commentary p. 196.

We give both forms of this three-part unison canon. For its complicated history, see the critical commentary and O. E. Deutsch, *Franz Schubert-Thematisches Verzeichnis seiner Werke*, new Ger. ed. (issued as a supplement to Series VIII, Vol. 4 of the *Neue Gesamtausgabe*), Kassel 1978, p. 92. The text (incomplete) had been used previously in canons by Caldara and Mozart.

Translation: I am tearful.

26. Wenn Kummer hätte zu töten Macht (Brahms)

Primary sources: MS, dated December 1867, Vienna; now lost. First published by C. F. Peters, Leipzig 1891, as no. 12 of *Dreizehn Kanons Op. 113*. Transcribed in *Brahms: Sämtliche Werke*, Vol. 21, ed. E. Mandyczewski, Leipzig 1926, pp. 186–7, with critical commentary pp. vi, vii.

The sources of this three-part unison canon are discussed in Margit L. McCorkle: *Johannes Brahms: Thematisch-bibliographisches Werkverzeichnis*, Munich 1984, pp. 451–9. The text is by Friedrich Rückert (1788–1866).

Translation: If grief had power to kill, it would have pierced this heart to death, and if some happiness had been allowed to conjure itself up again, my sighs would have suppressed it.

27. An den Sturmwind (Cornelius)

Primary source: *Drei Chorgesänge Op. 11*, for mixed choir; no. 2, E. W. Fritzsch, Leipzig 1871. Transcribed in *Peter Cornelius: Musikalische Werke*, Vol. 2, ed. Max Hasse, (1905, reprinted 1971), pp. 132–41 with critical commentary p. viii.

According to Hasse, a manuscript of this piece was still in the possession of the Cornelius family in 1905. In writing it, Cornelius did not adhere faithfully to the poem by Friedrich Rückert (1788–1866). Max Hasse has, as far as possible, amended Cornelius's words to agree with Rückert's text. We give Cornelius's version.

On the third beat of b. 110, the symbol over all parts presumably means that these notes are to be sung unaccented. (It is a sign that Schoenberg also used occasionally.)

Translation: Mighty one, who roaring bends the tree-tops, who swings blustering from crown to crown, wander forth and tear my stormy breast from me. Like the clouds that flee thundering before you, resting upon your raging force, lead my spirit from its mortal abode out storming into eternity. Lead me away where the failing world falls apart in ruins and devastation. Over the ruins, with awful delight, I feel the power of God beating in my breast.

28. Christus factus est (Bruckner)

Primary Source: *Vier Graduale für Sopran, Alt, Tenor und Bass*, Rättig, Vienna 1886.

Renate Grasberger (*Werkverzeichnis Anton Bruckner*, Tutzing 1977, p. 15) gives 28 May 1884 as the date of origin of this piece (presumably this is the date on the original MS), and tells us that it was first performed in Vienna on 9 November that year. It appears to be Bruckner's third setting of this text, which is not only the Gradual for Maundy Thursday, but appears in all the daily hours during the three days before Easter Sunday.

Translation: Christ was made for us obedient until death, even death upon the cross. For which reason God exalted him, and gave him a name that is above every name.

17–18.3 : tie omitted / 47–8.3 : tie omitted

29. Beati quorum via (Stanford)

Primary source: *Three motets Op. 38*, no. 3, Boosey, London 1905.

This is a six-part setting of a Latin translation or paraphrase of Psalm 119 : 1 that is slightly different from the Vulgate.

Translation: Blessed are they whose way is pure: who walk in the law of the Lord.

39–40.2 : tie between E flats / 68.6: *p* over 1st crotchet rest / 69.6.1: *p* omitted

30. Guds Sön har gjort mig fri (Grieg)

Primary source: *Vier Psalmen frei nach älteren norwegischen Kirchenmelodien . . . Op. 74*, no. 2, C. F. Peters, Leipzig 1907. Transcribed in *Edvard Grieg: Gesamtausgabe*, Vol. 17, ed. D. Fog, Frankfurt 1985, pp. 106–12, with critical commentary pp. 169–72.

The sources for this piece are described fully in Fog's critical commentary, from which it emerges that this piece is not a psalm, but a setting of a poem by the Danish hymn-writer H. A. Brorson (1694–1764), and that the 'church melodies' of the title are Norwegian folksongs, taken from a mid-nineteenth-century folksong collection for piano.

SIMON HARRIS